There is no better claimant to the title of Poet Laureate of the struggle for a better society for all, in this part of the world than Aj. Dagga Tolar.

Unrepentant as ever, is every line unmistakably a Daggaish commitment to the one vision of organizing the vast majority of the poor oppressed working people not to merely lament their plight but to collectively seize their fate in struggle, in solidarity, on their own revolutionary banner. Indeed on their own political platform can a victorious assault be waged against the continued misrule of capital.

This is poetry in the best of waters, the 'dark...' remains unable to smear or blemish the purity of the whole collection'.

Aj. Dagga Tolar is a song-writer and a Reggae artist, the publicity secretary of Campaign for Independent Unionism (CIU), now known as the Campaign for Democratic Workers Rights (CDWR) and the organ of the Democracy Socialist Movement. He is the author of *This Country is Not a Poem* (Kraft, 2006).

POETRY

ISBN 978-039-186-X

9 789780 391867

kraftgriots

DARKWATERS DRUNKARD
POEMS

Kraftgriots

Also in the series (POETRY)

David Cook et al: *Rising Voices*
Olu Oguibe: *A Gathering Fear*; winner, 1992 All Africa Okigbo prize for Literature & Honourable mention, 1993 Noma Award for Publishing in Africa
Nnimmo Bassey: *Patriots and Cockroaches*
Okinba Launko: *Dream-Seeker on Divining Chain*
Onookome Okome: *Pendants*, winner, 1993 ANA/Cadbury poetry prize
Nnimmo Bassey: *Poems on the Run*
Eberereonwu: *Suddenly God was Naked*
Tunde Olusunle: *Fingermarks*
Joe Ushie: *Lambs at the Shrine*
Chinyere Okafor: *From Earth's Bedchamber*
Ezenwa-Ohaeto: *The Voice of the Night Masquerade*, joint-winner, 1997 ANA/Cadbury poetry prize
George Ehusani: *Fragments of Truth*
Remi Raji: *A Harvest of Laughters*, joint-winner, 1997 ANA/Cadbury poetry prize
Patrick Ebewo: *Self-Portrait & Other Poems*
George Ehusani: *Petals of Truth*
Nnimmo Bassey: *Intercepted*
Joe Ushie: *Eclipse in Rwanda*
Femi Oyebode: *Selected Poems*
Ogaga Ifowodo: *Homeland & Other Poems*, winner, 1993 ANA poetry prize
Godwin Uyi Ojo: *Forlorn Dreams*
Tanure Ojaide: *Delta Blues and Home Songs*
Niyi Osundare: *The Word is an Egg* (2000)
Tayo Olafioye: *A Carnival of Looters* (2000)
Ibiwari Ikiriko: *Oily Tears of the Delta* (2000)
Arnold Udoka: *I am the Woman* (2000)
Akinloye Ojo: *In Flight* (2000)
Joe Ushie: *Hill Songs* (2000)
Eberereonwu: *The Insomniac Dragon* (2000)
Deola Fadipe: *I Make Pondripples* (2001)
Remi Raji: *Webs of Remembrance* (2001)
'Tope Omoniyi: *Farting Presidents and Other Poems* (2001)
Tunde Olusunle: *Rhythm of the Mortar* (2001)
Abdullahi Ismaila: *Ellipsis* (2001)
Tayo Olafioye: *The Parliament of Idiots: Tryst of the Sinators* (2002)
Femi Abodunrin: *It Would Take Time: Conversation with Living Ancestors* (2002)
Nnimmo Bassey: *We Thought It Was Oil But It Was Blood* (2002)
Ebi Yeibo: *A Song For Tomorrow and Other Poems* (2003)
Adebayo Lamikanra: *Heart Sounds* (2003)
Ezenwa-Ohaeto: *The Chants of a Minstrel* (2003), winner, 2004 ANA/NDDC poetry prize
Seyi Adigun: *Kàlákìní: Songs of Many Colours* (2004)
Joe Ushie: *A Reign of Locusts* (2004)
Paulina Mabajoye: *The Colours of Sunset* (2004)
Segun Adekoya: *Guinea Bites and Sahel Blues* (2004)
Ebi Yeibo: *Maiden Lines* (2004)
Barine Ngaage: *Rhythms of Crisis* (2004)
Funso Aiyejina: *I, The Supreme & Other Poems* (2004)
'Lere Oladitan: *Bqqlvkaja: Lagos Poems* (2005)
Seyi Adigun: *Bard on the Shore* (2005)

DARKWATERS DRUNKARD
POEMS

Aj. Dagga Tolar

kraftgriots

Published by
Kraft Books Limited
6A Polytechnic Road, Sango, Ibadan
Box 22084, University of Ibadan Post Office
Ibadan, Oyo State, Nigeria
℡ 234 (2) 7523177, 0803 348 2474, 0804 210 8712
E-mail: kraftbooks@yahoo.com

First published 2007

ISBN 978-039-186-X

= KRAFTGRIOTS =
(A literary imprint of Kraft Books Limited)

First printing, June 2007

To all those worldwide
Who live every day of their lives
Steeling themselves strong with the vision
That a new world of freedom and decent living
For all is possible as opposed to this present disorderly
World arrangement of disease, ignorance, illiteracy, poverty,
injustice, exploitation and oppression.

Appreciation

My appreciation to the *Daily Times*, where poems like "Songs of a deprived people", "The poet died", "We shall make them burst" had first appeared and *Vanguard* also for the poem , "Free to live without worries".

Sincere appreciations are due also to Rotimi Ewebiyi, now late, who initially urged on this work; Ronke Adebayo, who did the first typesetting of this work; Bisi Oladeinde; Okoro St. Louis; Adewale Bashar; Theo Alfred, who read through the manuscript and offered useful suggestions.

And not to forget Saheed Akingbade and Victor Osakwe for their timely assistance in seeing this publication to print.

Aj. Dagga Tolar

Foreword

Words pleading the plight of our darkwaters, pitched by darkness. 'Of our darkwaters and our darkland' bemoans us, still, not that we are back again into tyranny, but that we were never for once even free, except that the ruling class unable to maintain its hold like beforehand to contrive to employing subtle wares of marketplaces phraseology sloganeering in open fanfare their love for "democracy" and "human rights" – nothing whatsoever has changed.

The despoliation of our whole essence, the very source of our whole existence – continues touching on everything life – flesh, blood, the trees, the seas, the fishes, the rain, the season, the air, all without which we are not humans. Indeed they can not also be human, who took it upon themselves to deny "the messiahs" of others, only to lord themselves over our very will and need to free our waters and our land for our collective use, and become themselves the antithesis of our collective aspiration, betraying their very word of hope of a new rebirth, of a new beginning as we are the more drawn deeper into the abyss of darkness.

Our greatest tragedy, even beyond the farcial reappearance of the dead past (and its outworn historically confirmed failed actors) in our present, is the surrender to "fate" that claims itself Lord, as opposed to the material fact that human beings ultimately determine their own fate not singularly as individuals, but through the collective social group or class in the society, that we belong to or represent.

Our last word as in *Season of Struggle* remains, a demand for a return to our quest for the barricade, not to empower another section of the gangsters, but ourselves. For only the struggle of the working masses on their own political platform, flying the creed to abolish the rule of capital, and its blind quest for unlimited profit and replace it with the rule to meet the needs of the people, can we ever hope to be permanently free from darkness....

Preface

I

The artist who crafts art
To crawl after reality
Cannot by such art become an artist
If there is anything that art confers
On the artist it is the title God
To be God is not to seek after what is
Tailoring it to meet what the eyes see
But to ride the imagination to juggle what is
To make the head walk
To make the feet speak
Indeed art is a confoundation
And the art craft cannot confuse
For art is only the ordering of confusion
Of insanity into sanity

II

The beauty of words lies not
In the ordinary of every day
Commontalk on the streetwalk
But in the creation of new meanings
For as in procreation we live on
So also in the birth of new meanings
Can words continue to be relevant
To our world and to our needs
But if we go on living the old
Life soon becomes the bore
Narcissism creeps in to sharpen
The edge of frustration
Readying our world into the extinction
Of blocked darkness

Contents

9

DARKSONGS OF
OUR DARKWATERS

Into darkness

The world birth flesh for flesh
To birth the world into darkness

To ease the kill of our thought with stones
They pluck us free from our head
The stubborn simply gets sent to the soil

Our very hands do the tippering
In stark darkness to stack stones
Into our fill we cannot feel for fellow flesh

Drunk at dawn we done
To soothe stones into words to birth
Flesh for flesh to birth the word darkness

Tears tearing down

Tears tearing down from the sky
Hungering for every patch of empty earth
The eyes cannot see the sea
The wind goodwill to wet
Season of skin sunning

Homing away the land from the living
Eating flesh fruits
For the flood flowway
We cannot memory rain
The past dies
In the face of NOT before.

No landing atop our darkwaters

The head sings swing
Only to hang in trance

Come they come in naked teeth
To eat up our flesh

Leaving out little needs no soul
To roam in freedom

Canoes can row unwet on sand
No landing
No landing atop our darkwaters

Another Head not our head
Swings a sing for fear to reign on.

Waters without wing

Without wings water
Cannot fly to the sky
We know garbage
Worked on by age
Becomes the hang of the living

We who live on this dark dirt
Dream the coat of our own waters
And cannot rescue our throat
Only water can

So we drink to the death
Of our soul to soil us
Underground to mourn
Our waters without wings.

We cannot bail free

With shovels
We cannot bail free from death
Sleeping atop our waters
Every bail to earth

Roots death anew
Into the flesh of the earth
From which we turn to feed
Our need for water not to miss
Drinks — the mix

No filter
They would not sell to us
Without our letting them do more drain
To rain us more death
Atop our need for water

And the seamen

And the seamen
See the The semen

Flow for men
Before the foremen

Break skull reach
To teach

School we know sees
No soft can sink into the sea

But the outstretch of hardwood
Is thick certainty for good

The trees are dying

And the birds
The songs that call on us

And the Owl which paths the dark
To feet us to a good hunt

On the death of the moon
    Can no longer

The trees' no longer
    Amidst a mix mud of oily mash

The trees are dying
    We go without meat.

The freedom of a fish

The freedom of a fish
Our own fish's right
To choose our own death
Hooked to be cooked
Pleasuring the intestine
    Of humans
(- their own right to fishes!)
Is annuled by darkwaters
    As we float atop
Humans flush us like plague

And the fishers become the fishes

And the fishes the cast nets
Seeking souls for the fishes
Vain is the despoiled desire
Meat cannot come
Fishes we cannot do without

    The net we casted
For the hammer
    Breaking the earth
Only to feed our flesh for fish
    For distant faces
      Of Shell

We become the fished for fishes
    To feed
    And now we cannot return
To our nets
    We lost the art

And to buy from across
    We hammer the earth
All day to earn not enough
And no time
    To return to the net
We are the fished

No fish no hunt

No fish no hunt
And for what of meat
Meat takes on the tongue
Chew up the lip to lay
Bare the banner
The Red hurt of anger

And teeth cannot tell
Its anger
Without tongue
How words gather
Together the rest like us

Who without we
Cannot this war wrong
The anger
We turn to blood
Our own numbers.

For fishes we cannot

For fishes we cannot
Do without we do with the can

This can of beef's we cannot afford
This can of sardine sandpapered

Reading a date of tomorrow tocome
When it is a yesterday's gone

So we eat deadfishes
For death to digest us as fishesdead

Hunger cripples our consciousness
Unmindful we are without power

To digest death for fish

Our own earthwater

we cannot touch our own earthwater
we hang on to the sky
       to the RAIN

we cannot go on playing the ignore
it is earthwater wing
       to the sky

we hang on for water

garbage for garbage
we drink the same dark dirth
       of earthwater

pipe to the sky.

To think of a drink

To think of a drink
of clean water
Squeezed from the clear crystal
drop of my own tears
In this hell
Is to sin the sun
of our darkwaters
Who visits
failed suicide bid
with death.

Confessions of a true drunk

I prefer the heaven
in a drink drinking merrily
than the heaven in having
to go underground to worms
swamping wordlessly to noth-
    inghope a dupe

and jesu was just not iron
in 3days unready for eating
earns free about in flesh and bone
the same flesh and bone walking about
can only weary the wait of worms
        not to forget it

he never was was a word
to heaven unlike the heaven in a drink
drink drunk on the dance
-     go ahead

atopping our waters with darkness
   they alone now can party
with heart without earthspace
   no standing for feet to fence
we hunger back to dusk to our rot

       their only care
   is the flowing darkwater
only otherway is to selflesh
   fellow brother flesh
they like to hear the dance
of one of our own voice
broken chord of discord
tortured to confess in the cell
'we were going to fire the darkwaters'

27

sand drown the death of our future
in dregs remain of broken bottles
this is a drink to hell-unlike heaven
in a drink drinking merrily
          a dream
we cannot drink this darkwaters

We have lost our season

We have lost
        Our season
And we reason
        The lost
    On warming

So even our turn away
From the dark earthwaters
Faces us square with a turn around
To the same darkwaters
Clipped off its own wings

We cannot find us in fault
Who carpet-shield the waters
To turn the sun on its own rays
—   Shell

Without our arms oiled
Not all wash our hands off
We would not soil them
With darkwaters
Oil rich to packaged springwater
        We can drink.

The sun unable to eat darkwaters

The sun unable to eat darkwater
Turns its fire to flesh
Burning and blinding
All who eyes to the sun
Mail complains

So we return to heart
Rush to knee
Fallheart before Ransomed
On the cross

We sing in our tongue
In wait we hope unfailingly on miracles
To return our eyes to see
We promise peace
Longsold Longdead

And we cannot the art
Translate STRUGGLE in our mothertongue
Mothers themselves fall prostrate
Before the young
To save their flesh
And go on eating poison wind

Only for all to welcome
Death into our pants
Before the helpless watching deadeyes
Of the whiteflesh Ransomed on the cross
To our fallheart before it
We slave our very soul.

Redstains

They grow a river
Of all places in a noose
Feeding on the waters, oiled
By flesh sunk in the deed of darkacts

Ringlets of skull knotted
From souls of sowers' sick
Dead of eating smoke
Can drink darkwater

Pooling out of the palace
With which they wash
When they can no longer watch
The hearts they send to hang

They hide their own hearts
In glove glasses to free
Their conscience from
REDSTAINS

Reign out rain

The single unsameness
An obstructing beat of regularity
Of we wake the walking away
Of a yesterday a crawling today
Seeds into the soil of familiar reality
A bomb and gather we the pieces
Back again to multiply new manners
From the jaws of the donkey
Horsed to banter flesh on the banners
For an extra second of survival
Now reign out rain
Beating out the casual serene of dew
Their cherished sameness
Of daily dawn of peace
Splattered before the sun as stink stew.

Break bounds

When our darkwaters break
bound
Guns the first to fly
And we who before now
Helled in darkwaters like
ducklings
    In deadwaters
    No escape.

Where do we turn
To the same darkwaters
Murking all surroundings
Eating-up whole huts
    In braodlight.
    Of click shots

The speeching summoning
Waterworks to the screen
Only for the vision' special
effect
Not for we, the tears is for
the oil
    Lost
The very troubler of our
darkwaters

The story of the canoe

(*Helen C. Nwachukwu*)

I

Sail on the sea
I saw the canoe
I battle for the paddle
'Not a peddler'
cannot shy the lie
The ART on my lips die
As I surrender to the seawaves
Toasting me ashore
Unable to craft
The word:
LOVE—
IS A STRUGGLE AGAINST STORM

II

In the calm of my alone
I suffer to worship
The smile of your face
WALL
Around my heart
OYA
Goddess of marveling
BLACK BEAUTY
In expectation...
I remain SANGO
The subject and fanatic
... of your's love

III

ATROPHY
Me away on weary rusting my wood
The stray of the Blessing' star
Sails me back on lone to the seashore

To become the scorn of OLOKUN
SANGO I am the thundering HOPE
The LIGHT to life other souls
And my own soul' awaits a RESCUE
Mission to ever living but cannot sail
Without OYA the CANOE to safety
I remain on the hang
For yes for my paddle
To slap the face of OLOKUN

The forest in my heart

The forest in my heart
How can I see the spirit of words
To unearth all over again the art
I cannot find my way
All alone to the beginning dead
And me bolding onto life at edges

Your forest in my heart
Growing a mountain of heads
Makes me an ant
Crippling on how to creep
Than the barks of your flesh
Not after I have trod the dark

Eating my teeth to dislodge
The hunger of my baby-leg
Cool can no longer drunk me
Nor the icy hand of polar

Our own very sons

Not from the otherland of our darkwaters
But from our very heart
Not sons of extinct pyramidnuts
But the sons of our very flesh and tongue
Who puddle the paddle
Conferencing with us against our darkwaters
In the crystal clear of our darkwaters
They were the ones I saw
In flowering gowns of guineas
Barking out orders of "fire"
To men from distant
land of no waters
Brandishing rods
To hot our hearts to hell
Our own very sons

The otherland of our darkwaters

I have returned from a journey
To the otherland of our darkwater
True fatfaces rule them too
But many faces there too are lean
Streets there are bare
Naked as the night

There
No one hears
Another's cry of help
So many noises of need
So many ununited beings
In wants of common

Sirens of steelfaces standstill the crowd
Brokers the broadroad free
For passing porch cars in row
Hurrying the Head in haste
To keep the rest in battle to board
A yellow coffin on wheel

Civility in no passport
So I dump my nationality
I become like the crowd a Rushian
Only to catch my purse flying in the air
The cheers greet me
A marked face calls me lucky

Attracting the stretched arms
Of the gorroed coloured teethes
Crafting syllables with dried spits
Showcasing unbroken English as wares
These are their worst unluckies
Dispossessed of their very life

Not to forget the boys owning bus stops
Living on forcing fees from every ride
They cannot like we
Voice themselves against wrongs

Lost their very life
Thought dead to earning a meal
And so they keep the quiet
Only to go the quiet.

To forever free me from drinking darkwaters

I

How I managed with the waters
    Unseen back to the banks of our darkwaters
Will only do with a lie
    For truth would send throats to hang

II

    They asked
If I have heard of Ken
    I asked
If they have heard of our darkwaters

    They would not hear out voices
    But played me their songs of lies
Of bush people hatred for uncommon tongues
Of bush people hatred for machines
    The very beauty of modern civilization

They can't imagine that I would trade low

To speak a mother tongue-song
    In the midst of white faces
They showed me pictures of roasted flesh
    The reward of our 'terrorism'
On unprotected pipes.

    They want me to back their guns
They want a word of support
    For their guns for our good
To keep the pipes safe for all
    Just a word and that is all

    They reminded me of Ken
The good of life
    Why I must not go his path

Honour demands I care
  For my own people's good

And what better way
  Than in power with power
With power my people
  Would worship me
For they would bless my soul' Rich
Send my children' abroad
  Free me forever from
Drinking darkwaters

I need not return to see the shores
  Just say the word
  A word of support
And my lodge would be paved hills

To all there want of a word
  From me
I answered in three letters
  K,e,n.

Not all white faces

Not all white faces feed well
Unmindful of our hell
They welcomed me
They have heard of Ken
Of our darksongs of agonies
By the rivers of our darkwaters

    Of our darksongs
They have heard
    And with me
They went before the smoking pipes
    Arms in arms in songs

We must go on
Not like before alone

    But with fellow voices
Blacks around across and beyond
    Our darkwaters
Whites in the homeland
    Of the multinationals

Rainbow voices
    United with us
      To free us
For once
    And for all.

OF OUR
DARKLAND

Father meets son

(Benjamin and Bosede)

Go On With One Nation
Came the clarion call
The Man went to war
Leaving the Woman behind

When he did return
It was joy in the heart
The Woman had a son
Alive for him

The eyes swelled the eyelids
Could not hold the heavens
The tears came raining down
The first time Father meets Son

Home was no zone of war
Why this kwashiorkor, this rags
On the son, the money sent home
Not a shilling was given the Woman

Gone for the Nation
And they could not in turn care for the Son
If the Man had gone with the war
No one else would have cared

Living in the end

Orun maja, orun mala*

Human stray in a steady gaze
Of life nothingness. The desire
For a go back dies with the time
Gone by. Miracle is a dead bone
That cannot be cracked by a dog
And of no medical use whatsoever

Then is nothing works
Nearly the same as working is nothing

Don't and death would walk nakedly
Into your bone but to work is to with
Your own feet walk into the loving embrace
Of death. The soul is a commodity bargained
Out of the reach of the commonman

Orun maja orun mala

The madness of Newton
Counted us out of existence
We don't count in the beat of the rhythm
For nothing ever comes down that goes up here
You learn to grow tall and see if that would
Get you to the sky where the sales take place

Fly if you can wings were not made
For the commonman they were made
For the birds who won't forget
The tortoise's fooling they would never
Let go a feather

Then is nothing working
The same thing as working is nothing

45

The undertaker digs his own grave
If survival is not the reason behind
Is digging trade, Let him be told
That help is bedfellow to hunger
For these men passaging the grave
To the sky would all be back to say thank you

Then working is nothing
Nearly the same thing as nothing is working.

---

* The heavens tight, the heavens resolves

Us against us

I

Bones cannot walk
But they can falldowing
downing/falldown
Thanks to the rage
smoking flesh into ashes
And the bones await plucking
But the rest of us run
We run from these corpses
These corpses of flower
Sprouting rot

II
So we can kill ownself
Our forebear would laugh
Not even for the meat
We kill our ownselves
Trepidation of the tongue
What wrong

Punish words we would not
Our own fleshself like our flesh
In worst want we kill
And our wants
Like before the killings remains
To perish us more into peanury

III
When in unity we all can
Through thought act against
Our common not our commonself
Our common state
To blame for all the crime
That sent us against us

Ajegunle cannot cry

I
Aiyeyemi*
Song keeper of Maroko
Ajegunle cannot not cry
Hearing this song for a slum
Fashioned to bleed off inhabitants
Like they did to Maroko
They would inherit the coast of Badia
Drench them free of our every footprints
Then sprint they would, of the coast of Marine
Shudder a slumber as they erect
Vallies of castle palaces to nurse
Another Hollywood romance that would
End in the conquest of the beginning act

II
Aiyeyemi
Song keeper of Maroko
Ajegunle cannot cry, not
When feet has to be gathered
Soul seconds stolen to meet
The fear of a future, homeless
Without the hope of existence
As fellow slums, turn their back
Against fellow poor souls, unable
To accomodate any extral single soul

III
Ajegunle
Where would you then live like a rat
United by the hostage of hosts
Live in our once possessed corridor
Ravage for substances, speeding from sound
With thought only on me, no more but me

48

Ajegunle caught in the trap
Only able to raise clenched feet
To mount a landmark of direction
No voice would heed, cuffed
Melodies of a sad song of survival
Ajegunle
Dead, without a single soul
From the slum inheriting
A space of sand. Too precious
We are flung to rot into smell
Dismembered by ants and racing wheels

---

* Leader of the Maroko Evacuees Committee

When I see

When I see your eyes
I want to tear at the end
Another anger's act
And the face
Of bloody rain of red
Paints the earth
With the colour of your eyes
The pain to death
To kill not dying

When I see my own eyes
Growing the colour I fear to meet
I die the hunger for flesh
Outside of me
I eat my own lips
And my own face
Cannot then live in theirs
To share and spread the more
The pains that anger the eyes.

Here

Here
There are rails
But no trains
Promises come cheap
Like metro line
For easy vote
Sandwich note
Into bread

All we ever begin

All we ever begin is our dying
But we never dance to this kind of poetry
Even if we hear it to the end
It is with feet rooted
But we are not steel
So we grow
Even in our stillstate
We grow
Even those who cannot hear this poem
For the fault that it is not music to dance
I ask and when the sound to dance plays
Why do we die our dancing
If we do not all grow
In our beginning to dying

They murder meaning

(*Ijeoma Oguachuba*)

In slow ease chiselling
they death meaning
what they call ink
twist life out of lettering
murdering meaning murdering

you know your art
if you do why bring in your heart
tinkering away the old with a new
always they kill the genius — who knew
another way to make the world

They better your words to keep the old world
the old world of This Day
that other way is lostland of away
be grateful they retrieve your art back-to-place
sealing your name with a crown
to earn your pay you kill a frown

done with the murder
the carcass remains hangs your name
in a corneredge like Christ crown of thorns
if only I can make you commit your own murder
of walking away with This Day into the blasting horns
of sounds of crying dying our world of pain

is a world hungry for renewing
and your art surely would HELP

Enemy of our freedom

My art against
Tyranny remains a lasting
Testimony against me
I am against this LAND
I am against these PEOPLE
ENEMY of our FREEDOM
This bloody won freedom
I am going against
The freedom of the watching eyes
Of BIG BROTHER
For my freedom
To procreate my own thought
Into words

Is my offence, against this land'
When to non-existence is gone by,
This land is for all and all is for all.

Even if I offer my shadow
To darkness to die
So that they can no longer
Smell my presence
Can I run
Can I hide
From my own eyes
Would they no longer see
The death
Carcassing the soul in the midst
moisture
Would they no longer see

The hunger hung on the faces
The death of dreams
Self into beyond
The youths, for want of tomorrow
Filled with pains

Would my eyes not betray
When they provoke my thought
To procreate a new poem
Would that not be another testimony
In the hands of the STATE
I am against this LAND
I am against these PEOPLE
Enemy of our FREEDOM
I am against this RULE OF ORDER

My tongue dance

My tongue dance
To the blues of freedom—
Doomed
If rottening tooth cannot hold
The Dentist dead the dunghole
Hoist the flag

Tonguing more songs
Coursing on the celebration
WE ARE ON OUR OWN
We thought of the Root of Rot
The boundary bound up by blood
Let the Tongues 'talk'
They say the tongue our tongue
Now wear own flag
Mindful we all must
Keep peace!

The peace of my mouth
The peace of the land
When not a tooth
But the whole formation
Tempted still by Hunger
Cries for a Dentist

My Tongue must dance
To the sermon of the Rock
Warning Tongues growing little feet
Straying anger on race on the street
The Rock can still scratch blood
The very Tongues who carved songs
Against the noise of silence
Who lost fellow marchers to steeldots
To win us all the FLAG
They now wear.

Another darksong

The city fell to silence
Not a word
People who make people
Perhaps they would reappear
But people would they ever end
People run
But people make people run

And the end dies in a renewed beginning
Words crowd out
By the dance of the matchet
Who invent new letters
Craft in blood and fire
To make another darksong

Only painters can be successful poets

Today
Only painters can be successful poets
The figure of language no matter
The calculus, ends up
Speaking the same tongue
They would not hear:
'We are hungry'
But with painting
Even suffering faces would wear smiles
For who would hang a painting
Of hungry corpses of hopelessness
On a wall of scalping pains of moisture
Offering no second hand coat of waves
To the crossing contours of disfiguration

Philosophy of poverty for a painting
They would not hang, that they cannot
Afford you say "a piece of ART"

Not when it is the dream
Offering all reality denies
So when Writers conference to lament
The death of poetry This poem—
Is not a testimony against their meet
Because I am not a poet
Not when I don't live on words
The people cannot read
Not when they are hungry
So let the painters
Who alone can be successful;
Be the New Poets

Home coming

(Elsa Modupe Bishop)

you have emerged from the womb of slavery
into the blackheart of your fatherland
and thought a welcome party would herald
your home-coming, but alas this people
could be dark, dark also in acts

the earth they pulled wanting your feet
off them, you could never have stayed
if not for your father, for him you chose
to fight, what is his should be yours
you stood their darkheart and darkacts

they should know you are not white
that home is where the head finds rest
and what better rest can one find
in this coming if not home, let your father's
bones be restless no more, for you have won

his home-coming was not just to bite
the dust, but to restore the hearts
to its root home. That he did and
for that this country you can belong
another home-coming made possible.

I carry my own roof

I carry my own roof
On my back' spiralling up
So my head
Cannot into it withdraw for a rest
The rain beats me
The sun heats me
A colding fever spreads over me
My palms fails to heal me
My parade comes to a halt
On discovering
My testicles in sore
But the sun how do I get
Its shine into my underneath
I pray against another rain
But the falling night
Who can with words hold up
It cooling moisture.

The dawn cracks the face of dew
Into a new day
The leaf of my flesh fall
This falling rot of flesh
Is no seed
I cannot sow for a new soul
And the stones
I have chewed for meal
All this while hits at my heart
My head heavy downs on my shoulder
Eating up my neck
I can no longer take the pain
I go for the stones, but my hands
Pull out my heart into the fire
Let the stones' burn
But this roasting flesh'
Speaks not the cracking sound of stone
But the doomsong of a darkland.

The name of the country

Tell them I would live
And if I do not live
I would die
Tell them if I do not die

The name of the country would they change
It to knock
This sound of fear would it no more rage
Us with shock

Then they would go against the market—
Free
Fucking their own philosophy of existence
In the behind of a tree

I am not a reincarnation
I am not a resurrection
Jesus is not my name
To bear for them their shame

These lots know they are dodging millions
To pile up billions aiming trillion
The sweating before the screen
Accounting not against the scream

Of poverty forgiveness, when again
And again they would let us out for gain'
Sake to slaughter
Us to a ringing champagne of laughter.

Simply missing'

My heart breaks
Beats by heartbeat breaks—
They are after me
Wait man hurries through
Who is after me
My own me' after me

They run after you runafter
You till yourunafteryou yourunafterrun
Afteryou all by yourself alone
Alone by yourselfalone
Yourrun afteryou Not youinyou
But they in you use you to runafteryou
And as yourunafteryou. They are sure
To be always after you

Until you can't take it any longer

Jump into the sea the sea like Jonah
Jumps you out ashore back alone
To spill your own blood
They like it like free
To be free from blame
The blame reads in the report
SUICIDE they like it
Like you would like it
Not reading 'SIMPLY MISSING'.

I can no longer wait for death

Misery going it seems
But not going
Life coming it seems
But not coming
Everything life in me
Master struck by misery
And end would not come

I can no longer wait for death

My sky I stripped to my very soul
My feet I ducked into my only pair of shoe
Sold out to earn my fingers her last feel of cash
My head I hang out of the thought chamber
That I may become free to freely
Walk away from everything life

For I can no longer wait for death

DARKSONGS
OF DEATH

How death cracks and torments

I have seen death cracks
To pieces people who have lived
All in peace making nonsense of love
Life greatest object for one so dear
To be loved we never again can love

I have seen death torments
The soul of a loved one, denied
A loved son, husband, wife or friend
Clouding life out from their very inside
Until to death falls another booty

I have not waited to be told
But have grown up to see for myself
That death mends no bones but cracks
And eats up the flesh digging everything
Once life into dusty dust

I have seen
I have seen
   How death cracks
   How death torments
   All those who live

And I do wander my thought into hoping
How death would take me unable to plunge
Me into the deep of sorrowball kicked
Into a grave how death would come
How death would come
But death would come and I would be
Unable to see or tell, how death cracks
And torments you the world I have left
Which makes meaningless, even words—

The poet greatest love.

One long lasting smile

(Jide Garber)*

The laughter abound
Was from the undertakers
Use to the sight, they could not
But laugh, for that is how they feed
The pastor attempted one, but was not deep
Having said that always you welcome people
Known or unknown with a smile.
I have tried picturing that smile
But who could have known that the end
Was on its way, even that one Saturday ago
You last lived, you filled our presence
Your face we can no longer behold
Tethering edge as slipped through our dear hands
And who among us can ever be bold
To read out that platitude on the placard
Raised above even the laughter
Of the undertakers, that life must go on
For we know it has not gone on for you
Sickled in the cell
Who could have guessed
The agony the pains inside of you
That you have had to live with
All these years, life we thought
Was gentle, so did your smile impressed
On us, the fool we were, got us lost
Abandoned us in a state of shock
When a simple headache, knocked
To win for your soul a smile which
You had freely given to all, one long
Lasting smile to win your freedom
From agony and pain, killing in us a love
As we do to dust what is no longer life
And error or mismatch, a chance life
You did manage well, rest eternally

---

*   1973-1994

Can no longer fall on you

(Benjamin Atulute Ajayi) * (1938-1995)

The light
Can no longer fall on you
You are gone, gone out
Of this existence, earthening
The dust into the depth of the earth

Bedsparkling the shadow
That you can no longer cast
I fall to rest on the mighty
Seashore of thought lost
In memory of your every trace
Then I race

And cannot meet
With your body again
For gone, you are gone
Out of this existence
And the light

Can no longer fall on you

---

*   1938-1995

We shall make them burst

(*Sesan Ajayi*)

"Sesan has joined the conquerors
He has been made to rest
From the tyrannies of life"
(Rev. Adeleye Adekoya Tempo, 29 Sept. 1994)

You are not unsung
For every life lived is a song
A Poet life
Bridled in the craddled, a candle
Burnt out at both edges edging
Out of the path of the fireflies

Why weep
While we yet weep
When we weep

That your words may hang
No more in the corridor
But drop in to burst
To circumcise the womb
And fertile out new Poets
New lips

Am I not like you
Another Ajayi

Let them burst
Your every song of sound
Let them burst into our lips
That our souls may all be redeemed

And your freedom won in death
Would not become a vain wind
Blowing dust to concrete

Our blindness the more
Rest in the wholeness of 'God'
Who in the perfect goodness of his art
Rested. We shall not let your song
Be like man
—God' perfect goodness in rot

For yours is a song
For every living lip
Yours is a song
That would not die
That burst' behind
For every new Poet
Would lip it
Not lick it

Alive to aid your art
Your song into perfection
The burst of the fireflies'
We shall make it burst
Then you would not die
"... as we hear that people
dies as in other places..."

---

* (1959 – 1994)

Agba sha
(*MKO Abiola*)

Agba sha
The old fades
We know onto death

And tyrants
We didn't take for human
The suddenity shocks

Agba sha
And the root of our feeble laughter
We hope may grow stem root

As the sun
Free from the Dark of the glasses
Shines through the PLAIN

We celebrate the MOON
Certainly they would let it shine
To resoul our nation anew

Gloom face hangs on the PLAIN
Cannot rock the air
With the rhythm — a remix version

As the MOON
Shuns freedom without the shine
Offered by the plain

Like Agba sha
Death is smuggled into the bar
Sprinkled on a TEA

The man Dies
In the sky of their Blue bar
Dressed in chats with visiting stars

And the plain
Space through the Galaxy'
And reaches accolade

They shall be roasted
The smile of the crooking cock
In hunger would meal

On the death of my father

The mourning for him begins
When he hits the road home
Not now, the tears you see is a sea
Of put up pretence that crumbles
On the very surface. He acknowledges
His word too blunt cut to throat
Exchange between him
And the now dead
But not to the point
Wherein he wished
The dead dead

And I am welcomed
With a sullen sadden face
Dead to laughter on the lips
The dead though is dead
Changes no attitude
'He spent no kobo on me
And I spent no kobo on him'
So should it be, even in his death

And so he stretched out to me
The son, the expenses
That included not one grave
But two, one dug in a swamp
'My brother is not a fish'
He says, even if he is
Like the other brother intended
He sure did swim his remains
All by himself alone to a restful
abode. Sure father did it.

Afrika

(George Yemi Iwilade & Babatunde Oke)

They came with gun bullets and axes
To battle a man armed only with sleep
And they say they are men
But is that strange to AFRIKA

    The land of Bushghosts
    And bar bar barians

Why then did they come
To see Darwin in manifestation
Or to steal Black Gold, to steal our people
The SLAVES that built AMERICA
AFRIKA burns, knowing no peace
They came again with guns and bullets
To eat our land and sweat of produce
To feed Capital's fat Europe
Saved from collapse
AFRIKA they laid to waste!

    The cry of the majimaji
    The cry of the maumau
    AFRIKA MUST BE FREE

They hurried us with our familiar faces
If free we want to be free take the polity!
What good, when the freedom cannot feed the people
What good when the freedom cannot educate the people
What good when the freedom cannot give the people water to drink
What good when the freedom still have the people living under no roof

And our own familiar faces feed fat
Power us to ants crushed by the iron heel of jackboots
AFRIKA where the people eat hunger & sickness for existence
AFRIKA where warlords stir the earth

To market guns and dollars for Europe & America
And this boy, this man — Iwilade chose for a name AFRIKA
Because he wanted an end to the poverty
In the midst of abundance
He loved the struggle — and the Union
The stepping stone to the future
But OMO OLE said no
And together we shared the concrete floor of panti
in the struggle against the fees of Omo ole
AFRIKA would not give up the union
Nor even its Heroes — "Tony Fash and others must be reinstated"
OMO OLE SAYS "over my dead body"

Who is afraid of summarily dismissal
OMO OLE could scare the UNION
So CAPTAIN BLOOD spoke with the night

And came they came in masks
With guns bullets and axes
They came for AFRIKA
AFRIKA at sleep
Only to blood our conscience
To wake up wake up wake up
"OMO OLE must go" and we won
But the struggle remains
The dream for the land AFRIKA
If Iwilade must not die in vain
If Babatunde Oke must not be a waste
The struggle then we must keep
To make AFRIKA a better place for all
What better means than the struggle

For Iwilade and Oke don't cry
But for the land AFRIKA and its people
Cry for a REVOLUTION

---

* OAU 5, hoacked down by unknown assasins on July 05,1999, OAU, IFE.....

Again we cry

(For Moses Oisakede & livingstone Aroga)*

Again we cry
Not tears that soon dry
But blood, the loss not the death
We all with breath
Must one day
Pay
Oisakede can no more
With us march against the open-sores
Landscapping the summit of our bliss
With unending long hiss
We starve, thirst
When in abundance we are first
Because BOOTS place on hats in hand
Trade off our estate to capital-quest' stand
Swelling our future with permanent misery
With what lips do we tell the story
Of men freely educated, disbursing illiteracy
In fanfare of songs
Radio' clattering all day long—
"if education is expensive try ignorance"
What trash our right in race
For the same "Zombies", "Animal in human skin"

Who do not put anything to think
For all these to stop
You freely chose the struggle all the way top
Everywhere they raise their hellish hammer
In seconds' flight — you raised the banner
Always the banner and what manner
A disposition of quietude
How can one forget this attitude
Your face in Ife, I still can see
When for AFRIKA you steel your tears not to league the sea

For you knew that only in the struggle unlimited
Can a fallen comrade with honour be treated
For you — Moses Osiakede
I would put out of my heart the pains of your gone
That I may the struggle all through life be my gun
Course to end for all time, the sorrows
From all our tomorrows

---

* died Sept 30, 1999, in road mishap, on their way to Makurdi to plead the
cause of expelled sudents...

Would daddy dead heroine you

(*Slyvia Plath*)

You played with Death
For a rebirth
Not for another woman
For mummy you never minded
Who with her alive remained a stranger

And daddy with his death-you lived
Your loved — your love to a lover
Blind — so blinded
You were willing for your daddy
to become the woman
— the wedlock

What wrong
In the end the art
Carved your heart
On a slab
Unpleasing the daddy
Would daddy dead heroine you

Executive sirens of death

*(Hannah Odunola Alli)**

Making us mad with sirens
Is not enough
Not even when we stubborn like Ewure
So bullets must first like mad Malu
"clear jaggajagga commot from road"
For executive sirens to cruise the road

We who with our words of defy
Stretch our feet on street
Armed alone wiht our voices to battle bullets
We who with our woes of want unend
Filled you lips with letters splattered
On the frontpages against tyranny
- Your testament of struggle for this civil

Open the pages of the road
And read there our own footprints
Only now your rule fester gullies on the road
To erase every of our trace
As you do battle to enter into record-
Songs of everything done
Only to be heard on radio
Only to be seen on telly
Only to be advertised in papers
And what we cannot but use
Like the roads sings otherwise

We would not these guns again
So we let you be
Only that we must not even standby
And see how powerdrunk eats up the road
For use for themselves alone
Away we must be out of the way
Only that Hannah was not in the way

On this road of life for all
Made dark like the land
Only sirens bullying through
With gunshots to rest from us
One who knows *"How to be Happy"***
"live simple, expect little
forget self, think of others"
Only if they do, your smile
Today would still be with us
Only that your type of verses
Is no way to owning
A foreign Swiss account
When they "pray always"
For *"life...[to] scatter sunshine"*
On them alone

And to think it was another woman
That still your smile only to be seen in pictures
"keep your heart free from hate"
To heed this your verse
Is to weep for Atinuke Fadipe before you
Is to merely weep for you Hannah Odunola
And I cannot weep water tears for you
Rather my heart with hateful
For all those who to use the road alone
Bullet us into the beyond
Only in this kind of hate to grow
In more hearts of all of us
To struggle to keep
The road free for all
Can is my love
Memory of you.

---

* shot dead by a security officer who resorted to gunshots to clear the traffic to make for the convoy of the deputy governor on the 5th of May 2000.

** a poem by the victim Hannah Odunola Alli, The Comet, June 2000

A mere figure 26826
(Oluwatosin Adelugba)*

I see your many friends' tears
For you cut short from life
As sand takes the place
Of the colourful robe
Of Keke High School
You can no more with them
Wear the same uniform
Ending for you all schooling
Future fullstop.

Death ever without thought
Allows a mere figure 26826
Translate for Tosin these tears
Of you are no more
All because another figure AP656LSD
Would not pay the toll
So Tosin must pay with her young blood

I cannot like your school friends
Weep, I can only help but laugh
Hearing your death committed not only
To *"bad eggs"* but at the same time
To *"only God who can decide how
we can depart"* for I know that
Those who *"don't want you to come
          to school in fear"***
If only they rule us well, pay all
Who work well, to meet all their needs
No one not even figure 26826
Would dispatch death to earn a living
Then today, Tosin would still be with us.

---

* 17 year-old student of Keke High School shot dead by the police on the
   14th of June 2002 at Jupon, Iju-Agege, Lagos on her way home from
   school.
** Vanguard Friday 21, June 2002.

The bullet cannot tell a lie
(Nnamdi Ekwuyasi and Morakinyo Akerele)*

Barely one week after Tosin
We cannot say some "bad eggs" or
"God" again decidingly wills
Another police to aim bullets
Not straying but straight into
The temple not the tyres
As if death is the brake to halt the car
And then more bullets and bullets
Leaving Nnamdi breathless
Morakinyo not yet wordless
Still gasping

I meet with your blood
On the floor of the General Hospital
The hard scrub to clean rhythms
The sad song of the dying
Life of Morakinyo
How can this country
Still be asking for a police report
In an emergency - what hell
Where is the good old medical ethics
Of save life first, questions later

This is no concern of governance
But the news of an executive
Visitor unreserved apology is all
There is to "we care for the people"

What more that is how this country is
Making our very own to kills its own
Hope of a better future
We ask, what war, why armed men
To fire *'fire for fire'* against any Human
Even Robbers, so long would the excuse be

"the policemen only did their duty
the victims who were shot by the police
didn't stop when ordered to do so
because we are in a country
*where people dare the law"***
So says the police superintendent
Who says the bullet cannot tell a lie
When Nnamdi and Morakinyo
Are not here to say otherwise.

---

* *Both men were short by policemen at Road block ...*

Free to live without worries

(*For Sam Ojame*)

The earth can wrap
They cannot beat, no way cannot beat
The earth the earth one day would have them wrap
And we would rap "free
Free at last". Free
From the looters who kill our dreams

Without the Sam how do we psalm
Waiting hoping one day'— one day
Now with our own lips we leap
Ahead without our Sam
Without your smile without your humour
To see us through the bumps of the Van
At our dear Guard

The show still beat with stone of okuta
They are not out to down their house of glass
The same faces reign they reign & still rule
Our screen with tears of "Jesus also wept"
And they would not like Jesus go to Golgotha
Rather they cross for our throat another sonata
Feeding us with lies
And make out dreams die anew

The earth can wrap
They cannot beat, no beat cannot beat
The earth the earth one day would have them wrap
And we would rap — "free
Free at last, free..."
Sam is free at last
But your freedom from worries
Is no joy to our heart
The rain last season still burn our flesh
We now have to go lone on our own

But rest Sam rest free
And we behind, eating the silence
Of your gone, we cannot your memory
Forget, death or no death
We cannot, forgive, and live
This poverty forever
Rather we rap on this song

They kill our nation
Who care for more, for oil, than human blood
And put us all without our necessity
To go on living for them
We would keep up the rap˙
The earth can wrap
They cannot beat no way cannot beat
The earth, the earth one day
Would have them wrap
And we would rap—'free at last
Like Sam to live without worries

DARKSONGS
OF OTHER LANDS

Ethiopiaethiopia

Petals of spattered red
Amidst a grey of green
Ethiopia behold
The long of Afrika
Your yellow faces
Still read the Black
Bombs can't kill

"And you are from africa!"

They asked me
If I had ever seen an Elephant
If I had ever seen a Lion
And I said No!
A Giraffe, A Gorilla
A -- A Zebra
I said No!

'And you are from Africa!'
They are amazed
I am also amazed
That they still think
Africa is a jungle
Resort of animals

Why we are dark in our black

To live through a thousand endless nights
Without beholding a single day
They say is to be born BLACK
Black as AFRIKA where I am from
But tell me who made her who shaped her
Who forced on us the creed
The lies with which we live and die
Killing ourselves to live only for the self
Is it not the WHITE
Who say they can no longer be dark in their acts
When they still bound us till this very second

All the dream

All the dream
There is for blackpeople
In America
Is liquid —dark
In a bottle
Not free
we pay
To be slaved
To drink poison
To our heart content

And soon we like
Our homeland Afrikans
Eat our skin colour
Only we call it colour
Another way to milk
Us dead
And us bottom
—We remain

The city of God

The Jew without God
Marx is dead
Cancel without god'
Then the Jew
But remains can't recant
Go for God is real
Dance to the sound of the trumpets
Remember Rehab dares not defy
Mohammed
Against the sons of Japheth
With guns and bombs
Do you come dancing round their wall
With songs and harps
Jerusalem
Dressed up in black purdah
The city of God
And without the Jew
What is God
Rather the Jew without God.

Not the skin

You want your White
I bat for my Black
And pulses repelling not likes
Will sink into feeling
And out comes the Brown
In between

Can't go back to white
Can't right the Brown
A shade less black
"I am not another race"

Certainly not White
Welcome to the Blackfold'
Embrace

The trees of tears
Growing in the corner
Of your eyes
Tells the colour
Not the skin.

Flower for food

All that greening
Screaming on the street
Reaching out to flourishing feet
Who takes flower for food
They die

But the murdering
Breaking back and neck is
Not only for a while, like
Your placard angering on the street

To ego to add to the beautiful
Mind of your care
For life ...

Death is undeleted
We click on awfully
Just another word —
To earn the means of life

To you I offer this dream

To you I offer this dream
A dream that my own people cannot dream
Not dream because their hearts are not
Made of stones but of flesh and blood
Yes flesh and blood is their heart
And so they think their blood
Would mingle with the flow
If they spill the devil's blood

And so the dream dies

Maybe in you this dream would live
Maybe in you what would die is fear
Then you would be able to care for freedom

"Intact" this is exactly what peace is doing
To us my people keeping us alive
Without freedom and yet they wouldn't see beyond
The blood in their heart beating for life
When death is what the dream is against
But because of my people love for peace

And so the dream dies

To you I offer this dream
A dream that my own people cannot dream
Maybe in you this dream would live
Maybe in you what would die is fear
Then you would be able to care for freedom

Can't find the time

Can't find the time
The pen to paper this land home
And they trust me
To tell I am fine
All is well earning dollars
Only that I do not know
When I would send
My first hundred home
All I can now afford
Is a postcard
Which refuses home
In an envelope
Keeping fate with the faith
Of lies in sceneries
Words won't tell
Won't deny.

I receive a reply from home
The envelope edges not smooth
Gum loosen off
The stamp need not tell me
The name of my country
I know the poverty
Of our every make
The tyranny of profit
Milking the most from the less
I congratulate AMERICA
This land of opportunities
This perfection this decoration
Of ROT this liberty
Of freedom unable to free me from
Wants a protruding pregnancy

DEATH cannot abort

A new wanderer comes in everyday
Learns the language the finery from
The very origin of Alphabets
And then REALITY
In a world newly ordered
Kills the dream in broad
Daylight KKK on black back
Sex unreinventable
Stock lost to this hole
This hell cannot be home
The envelope the one bearing
The stamp bearing
The name of my country
I dare not dispatch dollar
To my people, living in the home
That chased my head
To this shattered expectations.

You who want to become like mobutu like pol pot

For us
The victory
Is in the end
For them what glory
Is there in the dust

Who celebrates' death
We do the millions
Of our souls sold to the soil
That the gun may over our head
Reign is glorious to our memory
At our today alive

So when the news breaks
That you too, the once ALMIGHTY
CONQUEROR is sacked by the soul
And reduced to remain
We do not cry
We celebrate this death

The people
Always outlive remains
Of Mobutu Pol Pot
And their likes
See why
We celebrate this death

After this war II

After this war
This war (2x)
After this war

Would the dive into the twin pinnacle
Be healed by splattering blood
The earth with teeth feeding on flesh
The sky raining bombs brothered
By the new manna of bread
With what lips would people eat
When dead sent to dust

Chorus

Can children now play it is peace
Will the ground not grow bones
To scare their littke feet
with raised epitaph
"This one was bombed here"
With no bush no Bin tc dump
Our forest remains
Questions arise anew
How do we explain away our earth
In infant stretch of seedlings
When the only play ground
Is the slab of death

Chorus

Ants ran mailing death
We run from our name
But life where is safe
The anger of a syndicate
Nurtured in buttered dollars
Comes down back with a heavy Laden

Would wrong ever right a wrong
Killing more the innocent common

Chorus

Would God learn to fight
Rescue his name from misdeed
Quoting scrolls to deny a people's
Right to land—
 Would Allah in own hand
Rewrite creed to teach
No honour in death
No life won in dying to kill
The innocent

Chorus

Will justice
Now grow in our heart
When machines still mint
Our sweat into banknotes
Our dirty hands can't touch
The coins we earn made barren
By market forces we cannot command
Then more would go without jobs
Without income— to live
More would die in wants
And hunger the anger anew
To rise allover again
And if we do not turn free
The hold of capital
For the reign of meeting
The people's need
Then again we would see
A new news of terror
For another war to spread the horror.

Anniversary of the fallen wall of berlin

How do we gather tears
For the fallen wall of Berlin
We who were children
Growing into manhood
Growing into womanhood
We who were born off the kisses
Intoxicated spirit of one Berlin
For a new humanhood
We along all those born
Today 9th Nov. 1989
And thereafter

Never saw the wall pathing Berlin into two
Free to grow to roam the whole of Germany
Free from the ravaging hits us back for Hitler's sake
Free from our own little little Stalin
This one new German nation
Born free with no wall on our path
Stalin endhome to the world of diktat
All these we say is past, but the present
What future for these growing children

Now that the eastway is Moscow
Who wants to go see Lenin's broken statue
-Stalin's apostate, no one we rush westway
Making the whole of East Germany also West

Why must we still slave to earn the fare to ticket
A crossing to the West to see all the screams
All the American' screen rush talkshop
Feeding us with a new future indeed
When we pay with our every sweat
In hours clocking in the sweatshop
And yet no living, so we do not yet pay
To hear swastika song of skinheads

Calling on new members to smask
The heads of new immigrants
When the Jews we harried to death
Scared to survive live to die Palestines
For a land of theirs to run from horror
For these others either way the tears
Never cease unmindful of the smiling
          potrait of Arafat

The fallen remains of our Berlin wall
Unseen by the lot is erecting anew
Binding this nation ever into two
We say let it not be for a new Hitler
Let it not be for a new Stalin
This present in between
Of unblueing romance of green rule
Is a dead carcass can never last
Not with Bush setting the world abush
Dumping terror in bug words of raids
Against the will of little nations
America acting is like making a new Hitler
Can we just talk and then stand aloof

Must we not rebuilt the party of struggle
We were the first, the greatest then
The way to go for all others, even Lenin
Only this vote for war credit
Lost we the way to the killing
Of Rosa Luxemburg and Karl Leibheint
The soulmates of Leninade Trotsky

Who is Stalin, Forget Stalin
When with struggle our party
Erects a new world for workers to rule
For all to live
Unlike then, this time, we mind our mistakes
No bureacrat like Stalin
For Lenin to die, to kill Trotsky

102

For when workers rule this laid
Europe also would follow in our world'
For workers' rule for all to live

Then the wall of Berlin
Truly would be no more
The tears, then would be
For the joy of a new world
Free from all walls for all.

POSTSCRIPT
FOR DARKNESS

Let him go and die
(*Efemena*)

Let him go and die
If we must go our way
Others must lose us on their own way
would you rather the dream die

You cannot, so why worry
When five letters would spell sorry
He would not take the pain
Would you rather you take the rain

Sob, beating the earth with tears
And live forever in fears
Unable to command the world
With your own care, run out of the world

You sold out to earn a kitchen
Life is not about ease eating of chicken
fists are needed in the fight to right society
wake up to this reality

for this dream
Let him go feed the stream
With his tears if you must have your way
Others for now must lose us on their way

Our own right of existence

Cats in my head
With their feet
I jump over walls
Eyes can't see
Wishing for the witch in me
They can't with stones
Dismember the word
Let them take the flesh
They can't chew me for meat
So I go on being the Rebel
Against their FREEDOM

For clean air
They earth the flesh
And what they have done
Is to have flesh become the earth
The soil giving feet means to move
The seed who mothers it to tree
The life on which they feed
The ENERGY giving the will
To become again the WORD

And the cat in my head
Grows anew
Disturbing their peace
I gather more of my type
On their rooftop
To nurture our seeds of song
In defiance of Bombs
Our own right of existence

The memory of the dark goggle

What remains
Of the dark goggles
Is the memory, which
Some want to dismember
We ask why
We who ate without moonlight
On the shape of vague' nothingness
Nurturing the dream of the dark goggle
To be ever drunk on Absolutely
The surrender to be absolute
They figured the finger in five faces
In the mirror we all could see
Only the DARK GOGGLE!

The mandate, the man, the date
The bar filled, they now killed
Let not mention names
The PEN begger words from the boot
"not again" we all
now scream
The very pillars' who stood the dark goggle
Are loudest of all
Now they are the ones
Who want to kill our memory
Arise and say No
Let the Dark Goggle live on in our memory
That we may all be the watch
On the ready to Arise against
Any Darkness— Goggled or Not
Our face beloves the sun
Only if our memory of HIM
We never allow to die

Bye bye to sunlight

A flood of sudden sunlight splashing
Does blood the darkest heart
With hope of a new dawn
But then the eyes
Used to darkness is deadblind
This new dawn going way wrong

Splashes sudden sunlight
Gives birth to shadows
A hide out for darkness
To bargain for more room
To roam free back to reign
Power in 'Ghana-must-go-bag'
Zip secured

It is bye-bye to sunlight.

Our soul' salvation

The blood of the soul' solves existences
Not the MASSES, not our own blood
To kill hunger with death
Dies the soul needling salvation

So die and water your blood
On the floor of our thirsty tongue

You cannot eat your blood
They cannot eat their blood
On us the vampires lives eternally
And we cannot reverse

To eat and drink' them—
Solution to our souls' salvation

Inhuman rule

Apples fresh, young
Lady-like would lend life
—the goggle
who was to eat was eaten-up
Here lies the remains
... to June 8 1998

The Hangman Unable
to sob the dumb Noose
Drenched in innocent blood
Now free to scream cries
How 3 letters like, K,E,N,
can go on living on the lips
out lasting the deeds of the Almighty
DARK GOGGLE

The streets joyed
we scream for 12
They schemed against June
A cup of tea to do the trick
Not we can get drunk anew
No new wine, but the very old
The good old 'Tested' "Trusted"

"To keep the nation one"

Of them like them
A prisoner turn-born-again
A rested Farmer's hoe
We watch the eagle go to the square
With an assemblage
of names —Ex-this

Ex-that, Ex-whoiswho
who have helped destroyed us till date—
These lots agree to a SNC
don't make me laugh...

Humans can do with furniture
3.5- in the behind cashing 5.5
And we the animals all unfit for N7,500
fueling us to pay more for fuel
And every other thing

And when in hunger
Awe turn to exist to eat our own oil
Hundreds of our roasted remain
at Jesse at Oviri

They placard to CNN
A deserve reward for our terrorism
on unprotected pipes
Always THIS DELTA
For the lost of 10 men
Rumbled down the whole of Odi
For another 19 men
sack Zaki Baim

>   *"Everything has been destroyed...*
>   *The town is completely destroyed*
>   *As I look around me there are dead bodies on the street"*[1]

But when the men
Go for there own strike
'Mutiny' rants the papers
Burya, Meigari, Idoko, Kyumgum
Arrested & detained
Animal treatment for all animals
They would treat us the same
After the Blast...

STOP DRESS
"Shut up you are being unruly
I am not suppose to be here"

And that indeed is the truth
Our president is not suppose to
Be president—

Is that why Safiya must die
1979 — 1999, 20 years behind
The march of morals

Women always wanting to woo men into woes
If Mallam Yakubu ate of the apple
Where is the swelling in his tommy
Lai ila, ila ila, Lai ila, ila ila, 2x

Flat down the cross
Roast the keferi alive
The East two begins to kill
Reprisal attack
Another set of poor,
The innocent poor always we pay
With our blood
Shagamu, Ketu, Ajegunle, Bariga,
Mushin, Ejigbo now Idi-Araba

We die we die

Why does death comes
So easy in this country
"Human Rights Day"
Citizen No 1 is too busy
Waiting for the voice of God
Our Electoral Rights taken away
Waiting for the voice of God
And we to be saved
On the judgement day

SHARIA RECOMMENDS —
"Stoning to death"

PadDyPaddy Government

Darkness amazingly lights
(Toikere B. Toikere)

At the doorstep
And I cannot find the passage
"Anything wrong" my flesh answers
Falls into the fire, my roasting
Issues rain from all my pores
Soaking up the sheet with shock
The rain misses the fires
The nakedness still in attention
Affirms possibility
To torch blood blood must touch
And me shying away from sin
Denying good to the flesh
Curses follow all the inhibition
"Get behind me saint"

The flesh is for sin

Pillowlost to flood
The flesh swims on the wall
Wet prints on the skin
Cool companies the state
Rest assured in pigeonholes talks
The nerve calmed I handover the key
The Newmaster urges me on
And darkness amazingly lights my way
Again to the doorstep
And the passage comes easy to find
My blood touches blood
Unsteadily though I learn
Art can only sin grow

The song of a deprived people

Let thunderous lighting strike
    Will the earth split
Let the sun smite
    Will darkness yet not reign

As mighty is your love
And almighty your God
Did our wishes not bear the nail
That pierced till death called

So let them be well and gluttonizes
Let their drunkenness soak our nakedness
Let hell that cometh forth from their hold
Baptize and scorch our bones

Do they bail out death
    To a sea content
Let them let them
    While they can

Yet — out of this very darkness
Shall our darkness arise
And when it does
Not one of them shall escape
For our darkness shall scale their sight

I shall sing of it
Because it is the very darkness

That shall bear our wishes
The very wishes
That shall stretch out for us a nail
The very nail
That shall pierce every inch of their flesh
From head to toe

116

Yes, yes
When that night comes
Let no one
Wail out a song of pity
For the sun has had its day
And darkness must rule the night

Prescribing more darkness

The new song—
"They came to prescribe the darkness"

How long lasting the ovation
No ending no landing
Permanently flying in the sky
Record holder—
All other past rulers combined

This philosophy to infest
The only way out
All the trust in US
And in one single' statement
Is made false

Ours remains a darkland
Spaced by darkwaters
The more oiled money
The less there is for us
What more to their new song
Than to shout down our darksong
—This doomsong
On the last page
On to another page—
The reality of existence'
Prescribing more darkness.

Kraftgriots

Also in the series (POETRY) continued